MW00627914

SOUL REBORN

A BOOK OF WORDS, MOTIVATIONS AND INSPIRATIONS

CHERYL POLOTE-WILLIAMSON

Soul Reborn
By Cheryl Polote-Williamson
Copyright 2016 by Cheryl Polote-Williamson
ISBN: 978-0-692-75480-1
Library of Congress Control Number:
2016909212

Cover design by Moyez Ibrahim Khan and
Crystal Manu
Soul Reborn is available on Amazon

CONTENTS

THANK YOU

Thank you to my first love God and to my supportive and loving family Russell Sr, Russ Jr, Lauren, Courtney, and Leah.

And special thanks to Keaira English for her contribution to helping me give birth to this book and Nikki Woods for helping me push forward.

FOREWORD

Over the years and throughout the peaks and valleys of life, I have found one thing to be true and consistent, my need for a fresh new daily dose of God. In the book of Exodus we are introduced to God's daily provision of Manna provided to feed the Israelites. My favorite part of this text was God's command to only take what was needed for the day. Some of the Israelites were disobedient and out of fear took what they believed would feed them for the next day as well. When they awoke the following day, the manna they set aside was full of maggots and spoiled. In Matthew 6:34

Jesus reminds us, "'Don't worry about tomorrow, for tomorrow will bring its own worries.'" This has been a clear reminder to me over the years to focus only on what I need for this day. God's grace and provision is all that we need for this day. He promises tomorrow He will renew His grace and give us a full portion of everything we need.

In Cheryl Williamson's book, she gives daily encouraging thoughts to ponder and consider that will help remind and direct us into a better way of thinking and living. One of the most promising tools of success is pouring into your mind thoughts that will increase your thinking which always leads to a richer business, relationships and peace life.

The beauty of this book lies in the daily manna that is just enough to feed you for one day. Each day, a fresh new portion is written as a rhythm to adjusting our way of thinking. My prayer is that this book will be a daily source of encouragement to those seeking to increase their thought life, which will in turn increase their richness of their life.

—Carla Shellis
Founder & CEO Sparkle Living Ministries

SOUL
Reborn

Saying no leads to so much
peace and more time for
God and you

Seeking the Kingdom is worth
losing the world

A positive mindset is a
lifestyle not a resolution

Show gratitude and thankfulness
by giving and serving others.

*A person in pain does not want to
hear how you fixed everything in
your life*

*Share your story; it
may help someone*

*Imitation is not always the
highest form of flattery.
Be careful and prayerful*

*Always make time to examine
yourself and your motives*

*Keep your spirit so high that
people's offenses and negativity
can not reach you*

When you truly love
people you don't sit around
and talk about them.
You pray for them.

You don't have to burn bridges
and you certainly don't need
to keep crossing back over
ones that have proven to
be poorly constructed.

When you know who you are you
become less concerned about who
everyone else is or is not

Focus on you

*Learn how to say no to
people with no apologies.
Your sanity depends on it*

*Always choose...
Love over Loathing
Humility over Humiliation
Righteousness over Being Right
Courage over Condemnation
Forgiveness over Fighting*

YOUR LIFE
has a
PURPOSE

Plant good seeds

*Don't carry your gifts and ideas
to the grave, Carry them to
the stock market.*

*God has placed everything
inside you to do what He has
purposed you to do*

Don't ever live so deep inside someone else's dream that you never fulfill yours

Use your test to testify to the glory and magnificence of our God

God provided you the wings of an eagle so that you can soar above offenses

Be good to yourself

Live a life poured out for Jesus Christ

There is a message in the misery
There is triumph in the tragedy
There is better in the bitter
There is peace in the pain
There is discernment in the
destruction
There is humility in the
humiliation
And God is in it all

Three tips to improve the quality
of your life
Positive Thoughts
Proper nutrition and exercise
Prayer/Gratitude/Thankfulness

God woke you up on purpose
with purpose

DO YOU KNOW
what God says
ABOUT YOU?

*Sometimes you must take a
break from everything and
everybody and just love on you,
encourage you, pour into you,
and be good with that decision*

*Your past is just a chapter in
your book not your whole story*

*Success comes when you invest in
yourself and invest in others*

You always have a choice
What you choose, will determine
your outcome

Sometimes you must step
away from everything and
everybody so that you can
truly hear from God

Everything you need to fulfill
your purpose is inside of you

You can't win against someone that
only competes with them self

When God is for you the whole world against you is of no consequence

Your fall is a lot more graceful when you have helped others climb

Everything you need to change is already inside you. Just do the work

Practice listening. It will help you really hear what people are saying even when they are not saying anything

*The best advice you can
give in some cases is none.
Just listen and be quiet*

*Choose your friends wisely
because everyone's heart is
not pure*

*Just be present; you don't
have to have an answer
or solution*

*There should be a place within your
heart where only God dwells
Meet Him there daily*

When you figure out how important a relationship with Christ really is you will never be the same

Meekness is not weakness by any stretch of the imagination

Forgiveness is really about you

Sometimes you just need to be present, be quiet and just listen

Give yourself away so God can really use you for His will and His glory

If you don't want to praise
Him that's fine but please
refrain from doing things
that hinder others

Whatever you plant and sow
into people's lives you will reap
and harvest in your own

Love yourself enough to
focus on you

The answers you are looking
for will not be found in "me"
time. They will only be found
in "we" time (you and God)

*Knowing, believing, and living
the truth is what makes you free*

*You are unique and you have a
purpose*

*Celebrate other people's
success and then you will
have more of your own*

FORGIVENESS
Frees You

Focus on improving you

Release yourself from the victim mentality and begin to live as a victor

The power you're trying to activate is called faith

Be present
Be intentional
Be authentic
Be a blessing

Find at least one person you can encourage today

IT'S TIME
to Change

Discounting and discrediting other people's dreams will not make yours a reality any quicker

God promised us a life of abundance however we are the ones that struggle with walking this out and believing it

Real change takes place from the inside out. You must be willing to do the work

Real growth begins when you
leave your comfort zone

Stop waiting on people to give
you permission to be great
It's already inside of you

Sometimes you are forced to pull up
what you have planted because
you are fearful of the harvest

Cover not Covet
Collaborate not Compete
Love not Loathe
Trust not Taint
Lift not Limit
Support not Scheme

Life is not about what you have
it's about how much you do with
what you have for someone else

A lie will never become truth no
matter how often you repeat
it to yourself

Make time to praise God
and serve His people

Speak life into someone today.
The world has enough critics.
Learn How to encourage people

Life is wonderful once you
release, reveal, and remove the
author of confusion and lies

*Be a blessing to others and
yours will follow naturally
I Challenge you to try it*

*Stop dimming the light God
placed in you to make other
people comfortable. That's why
they make sunshades*

*I pray for you, you pray for me and
watch God change things*

*Stop begging and
pleading with God and start
thanking and praising Him*

*It's not always other people,
envy, jealousy, haters or the
devil, it's you plain and simple.
Get out of your own way*

*Brokenness is a condition. It's not
an excuse to seek to break others*

*Worship God in earnestness
and truth and you will see
your circumstances change*

*Be still and know that
He alone is God*

World, community, family, self, God
Change the order and your
life will change
God, self, family, community, world

Gossip is not prayer

If you really want to be a
blessing to someone today
Don't ask
Don't advise
Don't suggest
Just be present and listen

Fear will keep a grip on you
as long as you keep a grip on it

*Let's join together in a complain
free week starting today
Instead of complaining plug into
Gods power and recharge
your batteries
Focus on gratitude, thankfulness
and serving others*

*You don't have to remind people
of their past because they lived it
Spend your time self-reflecting.
That's where real change begins*

*Don't continue to walk
around with unopened gifts.
Your destiny Is waiting*

Make an appointment to enjoy you

Pay it forward today by smiling at someone. Avoid confrontation by praying instead. Pay someone a compliment or leave someone a note with a cheerful message The cost to do this is zero. The reward can change the outcome of a generation

God sees the best in you. Don't you think it's time for you to see the same thing

WITH GOD
all Things are
POSSIBLE

*Leave all the outcomes
to God*

Allow God to truly use you

*Take God out of the box and
impossibilities will become
possibilities.*

*Your dreams don't have an
age to fulfillment*

God has the power to rebuild the broken hearted

Dealing with pain is not a one size fits all

If you believe the promises of God, move forward with what He has placed in your heart Leave all the outcomes to God

If we plant the right seeds in people, God will help them grow

Do not be deterred, be determined

Your dreams will only be as big as you think they can be
Dream BIG

IN THE
Storm

*It's impossible for someone to
lead you out of darkness when
they can't see themselves*

*God can take total disaster
and turn it into victory*

*Believe in God when you don't
believe in yourself or anyone else
His promises are true*

*Peace comes when prayer
and praising begin*

God understands
a moan and groan
He is an awesome interpreter
of his children's silence and
signals and nonverbal
communication

Surrender simply means you trust
in the promises of God and you
know you cannot do anything
within your own power

Rest well tonight knowing
that nothing catches
God by surprise

*The test is for you and the
testimony is to glorify
God and help others*

*Stop wondering and worrying
and start worshipping
and praying*

*The position for any battle is
on your knees*

*In order to experience the peace
sometimes experiencing the pit
will become necessary. Focus on
the palace to get out of the pit.*

Things I learned in the desert

- *Stay in the word*
- *Leave your burdens at the master's feet*
- *Know who your friends are and are not*
- *Allow God to handle those who negatively contribute to your desert season*
- *God is powerful*
- *Forgive anyone that has wronged you*
- *Only God can change your circumstances*
- *Gods timing is perfect*

- *Man's opinion of your circumstances really does not matter*
- *Some people are happiest when they think you are struggling*
- *Love God on the days you feel you can't even love yourself*
- *Your enemies should be kept at a distance*
- *Trust God not matter what*

Expect a blessing in the breaking

Release your pain and power through your pen

The peace you are searching for can only be found on your knees

THERE IS
Purpose in
YOUR PAIN

There is growth from grief
Humility in heart break
Deliverance from deceit
Breakthrough in betrayal
Smiles from sadness
Patience in pain
Way out after wandering
All this happens only
when we trust God

Sometimes exposing your pain
will help someone get
through theirs

The misery may very well turn
into your ministry

The worst attack of the enemy
can become your greatest
testimony to who God is

There is a plan and
purpose in all the pain.
Keep trusting God

Lord help us to deliver our stories in a way that will heal wounds, ease pain, and set the captive mind and soul free. In Jesus name

LEARN
to be
STILL

Silence can be a
powerful message

Listening is the answer that
unlocks the truth, hurt and pain

God is breaking you to
build you into exactly what
He wants you to be.
Stay the course
He is almost done

*God can use anybody and
so can the devil*

*Pray about everything and
everybody*

*Stay in the moment
it's all you have*

AFFIRMATIONS

I'm on fire for Jesus.
Move or be burned

The two dates I love the most are
the day I was born and the day
God showed me why I was born

God is essential and eternal
Everything else is extra

It's best to work alone than
be in bad company

You alone are God

Today I am grateful for
restoration provision,
peace, and grace

Look in the mirror and
say it to yourself
I am forgiven
I am beautiful,
I am intelligent,
I am employed,
I am healthy
I matter in this world
I am at peace with my enemies
I am debt free
I am living my purpose

God is real and so are His promises

Today I forgive myself for not trusting that God had placed everything in me to fulfill my purpose and destiny

The best kept secrets are the ones between you and God

Let go and let God

If Heaven is anything like I Imagine I sure want to do everything God has asked of me to experience it

Love, Forgive, Trust Me

Connect with the Author

Cherylpolote-williamson.com/
Email: author@cherylpolote-williamson.com
Twitter: CherylPWSpeaks
FB: https://www.facebook.com/
groups/1796622886607798
Mail: 6101 Long Prairie Road Suite 744,
#269 Flower Mound TX, 75028